The
Connection
Process

The Connection Process

A spiritual technique to master
the art of relationships

Teal Swan

ARCHWAY
PUBLISHING

Archway Publishing books may be ordered
through booksellers or by contacting:

Archway Publishing
1663 Liberty Drive
Bloomington, IN 47403
www.archwaypublishing.com
1 (888) 242-5904

Because of the dynamic nature of the Internet, any web
addresses or links contained in this book may have changed
since publication and may no longer be valid. The views
expressed in this work are solely those of the author and do
not necessarily reflect the views of the publisher, and the
publisher hereby disclaims any responsibility for them.

Any people depicted in stock imagery provided
by Getty Images are models, and such images are
being used for illustrative purposes only.
Certain stock imagery © Getty Images.

ISBN: 978-1-4808-6115-2 (sc)
ISBN: 978-1-4808-6116-9 (e)

Library of Congress Control Number: 2018907035

Print information available on the last page.

Archway Publishing rev. date: 6/15/2018

Contents

I.   Connecting With Your Heart............................ 1

II. The Octopus Technique 7

III. The Connection Process....................................13

a.   Introduction to The Connection Process...........13
b.   Walls 24
c.   Landscapes.. 38
d.   What Is Beyond the Walls and Landscapes? 45
e.   Unconditional Presence 48
f.   The Missing Mirror..51
g.   The Connection Process Steps........................... 54
h.   Performing The Connection Process with
     Yourself.. 63
i.   An In Depth Example of The Connection
     Process – The Cave Within 71
j.   Connecting with Body, Emotion and Mind 88
k.   Connection as our Lifeblood 92

All pain in this universe is initiated by some kind of separation. Our birth into this life and into this world is through separation; separation from our source, separation from our essence, separation from our mothers, separation from ourselves, separation from what we fear, separation from what we love. This continues until we find ourselves disconnected and deep in the torment of isolation. But we are initiated through separation so that we can find our way back to connection.

All pain in the universe is initiated by some kind of separation and all joy in the universe is initiated by some kind of unification. The main suffering that human beings experience on this planet is that we walk this earth with multiple billions of other people and yet each of us feels alone. Because of the trauma of our own disconnection, we perceive ourselves to be disconnected from anything we see as "other". This pain of disconnection spreads out across this planet like a cancer.

Connection can be thought of as a **link** with something else. Connection can exist at any level of our being. We can be mentally linked, emotionally linked, energetically linked and/or physically linked to something. When we disconnect, we break that link we have to another person on whatever level we disconnect, if not all levels.

At the most fundamental level, to love something is to take it as part of yourself. It is an experience more than it could ever be a concept. Love is inclusive. It is the energetic movement towards oneness. When you connect with something so as to love that something, you energetically pull it towards you and include it as you.

If you are truly connected to something, you cannot cause it pain without causing yourself pain too. When we perceive ourselves to be disconnected, we no longer feel the ripples in the oneness that is our fundamental truth. We no longer feel the impact that everything has on us and that we have on everything else and as a result we can cause something pain without perceiving that pain in ourselves. This condition leads to a world that is not conducive to any life, much less human life. This is why re-establishing a sense of connection among us is no longer a luxury, it is a necessity. The survival and thriving of our individual lives, our species and more than that, our world is dependent upon it and it is in the re-establishment of our connection with each other and with 'other things' in the world, that we will bring about the happiness and harmony that we seek. It is in the re-establishment of our connection that we will create the new earth.

This book presents 3 powerful esoteric processes, culminating in the process that I call **The Connection Process.** These processes restore you from a state of separation, to a state of connection both with yourself and with other people. These processes will enable you to perceive the fundamental truth of yourself as well as the fundamental truths belonging to other people. They will enable you to perceive fundamental truths that exist far beyond the tangible physical dimension. These processes will enable you to see, hear, feel and understand yourself and other people and the result will be a deep sense of connectedness with yourself, with others, and with the world.

Connecting With Your Heart

Our bodies are more like eco systems than organisms. There are a great many beings that call your body home, such as microorganisms and bacteria. These beings are indivisible from you because they benefit your existence and you could not exist without them any more than they could exist without you. What many people do not know is that your cells and organs are also more like separate beings that call your body home. We have the tendency of viewing them as if they are machine like parts of ourselves. In truth, they are indivisible from you, but they also have their own consciousness and personalities. *You,* (the you that you call by your name) are really the collection of all of these things. You are in essence a small-scale collective consciousness.

Understanding and beginning to view your body in this way is really important because so much health and vitality can come as a result of connecting with and honoring the separate parts of the ecosystem that is your body. One of the most important parts of your body to connect with is the heart. When I refer to the heart I am referring to much more than just your physical heart that is beating in your chest. That is only the physical aspect of your heart. Your heart, just like every other aspect of you, is multidimensional in nature. Your heart can be thought of as the center of your being, the center of your personal essence and therefore personal truth.

The heart is the first organ to form when the body is developing in utero. When an embryo is made up of only a very few cells, each cell can get the nutrients it needs directly from its surroundings. But as the cells divide and multiply to form a growing body, it soon becomes impossible for nutrients to reach all the cells efficiently without help. The cells also produce waste that they need to get rid of. So the heart and the blood and circulatory system that branches off from the heart, form the first organ system to develop in the human body. The heart is the connection between all future systems which comprise the body. This is why it is so often seen as the center of your being. You can use the heart as a doorway between physical and non-physical reality. It is the main doorway between your soul and your physical body. You can also use the heart to send energy to all parts of your body (much like it sends blood to all parts of your body).

I want to introduce you to an exercise that you can use in order to connect with any part of your body, but for this exercise, you are going to use it to connect with your heart.

To begin, close your eyes and place your hands, one on top of the other, over the top of your heart. Your heart is located right beneath your sternum in the center of your chest. Take some time to feel how your heart feels to you on both a sensation level and on an emotional level. If I were to mention the name of one of your friends, you would notice that there is an accompanying sensation that comes along with your idea of that person. This, more so than their name or details about them, is their *signature*. This is how your being recognizes them as different from the rest of the people you know. Your heart is like a friend, a friend you probably don't know very well yet. But it has it's own signature just like your friends do. This is why you can feel it as a being inside of you with a very specific life's purpose to fulfill ... namely to keep you alive.

Imagine your heart as a separate being that lives inside you. What does your heart feel like? What does it appear as? (perhaps you will visualize your heart as an actual mini being or even as a mini person at this point). If your heart were a living being, what personality would this being have? What would this being want? What would this being dislike? Does this being feel appreciated and loved or does it feel ignored and undervalued?

Just take some time to be with your heart exactly as it is and exactly how it feels right here and now. There is no right or wrong way to have a conversation with your heart. You intuitively know what kind of conversation needs to take place. But I will give you a basic outline for developing a 2-way connection with your heart. Begin by asking your heart directly, "What makes you unhappy?" "What do you need me to do differently?" "If you could have one wish, what would it be?" And "What do you have to tell me?" You will receive the answers on an intuitive level. Either you will hear the answers or you will see them in your minds eye, or you will find that you just know the answers intuitively because they will pop up in your consciousness. Imagine or sense or feel your heart talking back to you in response to your questioning, just like another person would answer your questions.

Next, it's your turn to speak to your heart. Address the concerns that were put forth by your heart. Acknowledge that you value your heart's needs and wants and perspective. After all, it represents the perspective of your true self. What do you think your heart needs to hear? Tell that to your heart. You can speak to your heart inside your mind's eye if you do not wish to speak out loud. Next, take steps to fulfill the wish that your heart expressed. Keep in mind this might not be something that can be accomplished in one sitting. It might for example be a lifestyle change that your heart wants you to make.

Once you feel as if you have reached an understanding with your heart, take some time to express gratitude for your heart. Acknowledge the work that it is faithfully and loyally doing to keep you alive and vital because it loves you. Express the love you have for your heart. Visualize that love flowing into your heart and nourishing your heart. See your heart sucking this love up and pumping it through your arteries and veins throughout your entire body. Feel your body as it too soaks up this love that the heart is pumping to it. Watch that love diffuse throughout your whole body and throughout each tiny little cell.

Just before you come back to the present moment, make a promise to your heart (if you feel ready) that you will always be available to talk to if it wants or needs to talk to you and that because you love it and have gratitude for it, you are going to fulfill its wishes because you agree with its wisdom and perspective. Then, take four deep breaths, allowing the oxygen to completely fill your lungs and completely exit your lungs and when you are finished, open your eyes.

Now that you have established this connection, make a practice of 'checking in' with your heart regularly, especially when you feel a strong emotion or have to make a decision. The more connected you are with your heart, the more connected you are with your own personal truth and the more connected you are with your soul. Your heart bears the burden of the emotional trauma that you have experienced throughout your life. Relieving that burden and expressing love and gratitude for your heart is a critical part of your spiritual progression. You are in a relationship with your heart.

Your heart is your best friend and it is your life partner. If you want yourself to thrive, you have to treat the relationship with your heart like you would treat the relationship with your significant other.

Having this relationship means that you always have someone to check in with and to consult about your life who always has your best interests at heart because it is in essence the core of you. This is what you need other people to connect to. This is what you need to be able to share with others in order to create a genuine connection and in order to share it with other people, you need to be aware of it and connected to it yourself.

The Octopus Technique

Chances are if you are reading this book, you are old enough to have a developed ego. You have a sense of yourself as a separate self that you call by your name. You define yourself by your beliefs, your likes, your dislikes, your past experiences and your current perspective. The problem is that this identity becomes so solid that it becomes like an egocentric bubble. We perceive other people through our own filters. It becomes very hard to relate to people who are different to us. We begin to project our own perspective onto them. When we are practicing empathy, instead of stepping out of our perspective and into their shoes, we take our perspective *into* their shoes. So, even though we may see solutions they don't see, we don't accurately see or feel them.

In order to exit our own reality and to be able to enter theirs, and by doing so completely attune to them, I want to teach you a technique to use. I call it The Octopus Technique. We, as physical beings are extensions of Source consciousness or what many people call God. We are Source manifesting physically. To conceptualize of this, I want you to imagine an octopus. The head of the octopus represents Source - a united oneness, sort of like a blank slate of potential energy. The legs of the octopus represent aspects of that united oneness extending down into a human body. So, I am a leg of the octopus and you are a leg of the octopus. For this exercise, you are going to use this symbolic image to get into someone else's perspective.

To do this exercise, close your eyes and observe your breathing. Feel your thoughts bouncing around and just let them do that until they slow down. When you feel ready, imagine your consciousness or soul retracting back up your leg of the octopus and returning to Source consciousness (the head of the octopus). As you do this, imagine leaving your identity in this life behind. See yourself leaving the story of your life all behind will all the people in it, your beliefs, your likes, your dislikes and your past experiences. Feel yourself stripping free of them so as to return to Source. Feel what that spacious potential energy feels like.

Then when you are ready, think of someone whose perspective you would like to see. Hold them as your focus and imagine finding the leg that extends from the octopus head (Source) you are in down into their embodiment.

Imagine, sense or feel yourself going down the octopus leg into their perspective, completely having left yourself behind so all you are now is the consciousness who is feeling through their body and seeing through their eyes. Imagine opening your eyes AS them. Imagine smelling as them and tasting as them and most of all, feeling the emotions they are experiencing. How does it feel to be in their body? What are you thinking in their body? See if you can feel their past experiences and how those experiences are shaping their current perspective. If you are wanting to understand exactly how they experience a specific situation, let yourself live or re-live that experience AS them. Feel and see the difference between how they experience life and how you used to experience life when you were you.

Spend as much time completely immersing yourself in their perspective as deeply as you can. If you experience emotional reactions as a result of it, surrender and let it happen. Gain as much understanding and awareness as you can. BE them until you feel a sense of emotional, mental and physical comprehension. Then when you are ready, imagine retracting once again back up the octopus leg into the head of the octopus (Source). But this time take your comprehension of the person whose perspective you went into, with you. Carry that comprehension and experience back down the octopus leg that extends to your perspective in this life. Feel yourself carrying that full awareness and understanding as you come back to your own life and when you are ready, slowly open your eyes.

All you need to know about the other person and

about what to do relative to them will be revealed as a result of doing this exercise. Your awareness will multiply and your perspective on so many things will change. So be brave enough to leave yourself behind. The more often you do this exercise, the better you will get at disidentifying with yourself so as to identify with someone else's perspective. Soon, it may not be a visualization, it may in fact graduate to a full blown out of body experience. When you come back from the exercise, ask yourself what was their perception of what happened? What was troubling to them about what happened? What were the emotions that they felt at the time it happened? What emotions are they feeling in this exact moment? What do they really need from me?

Think about how good it would feel for someone to completely understand you. Think of how good it would feel to be able to have them be so perceptive of your internal world that they know exactly what you need and exactly what to say. Think of how good it would be to have harmony in your relationships instead of conflict and for your relationships to feel secure and safe. This is the kind of relationship that is available to you if you practice attunement with one another.

If you are not naturally attuned to the people and things around you, you will have to consciously think about attuning. You will have to practice it in the same way that someone has to really concentrate to do the backstroke when they first start swimming. But with enough repetition, it will become natural to you. It will become second nature and the disconnected, isolated, individual reality that is in denial of the world around it, will begin to feel like what it is, a prison. You will see that instead of the place that keeps you safe, it is the place that keeps you and the world around you unsafe.

The Connection Process

Introduction to
The Connection Process

Imagine that you are living in the 1860s. No man has ever managed to penetrate the deep seas. In fact, deep-sea exploration is a brand new science. Being the first deep sea explorer, as you stand on the shore looking out over the expanse of the ocean, you have no idea what you will find down there. You have no idea how deep it goes. You have no idea what life forms live there. You have no idea if there are entire other worlds down there. You have no idea if you will survive your explorations. All you know about the ocean is what has washed up on the shore. All you know are stories from fishermen about what might be down there. Your imagination and curiosity are your only allies in this exploration. Your guide is nothing more than your desire to see, to feel, to hear and to understand what you will find down there.

I want you to imagine for the sake of this process that each person has a universe inside their own skin. These universes are not small, they are as large as a typical universe. The fact that this universe fits inside a human body is simply a trick of perception in our physical world. Most people never explore their own internal universe, much less anyone else's. Our inner worlds remain untouched and this is the pain of our lives. So, going back to the first analogy I used, I want you to imagine that when you meet someone new, you are standing on the shore of an ocean that has never been explored before. You are in the very same position relative to this person that the very first deep-sea explorers were in relative to the actual ocean. They were about to start an exploratory process, having no idea what they might encounter. The process of intimacy in a relationship is the process of going deeper and exploring more of that ocean within them.

Because every person has his or her own universe within that is completely unique, I could never tell you what you will find inside a person. I could never tell you what you will definitely see or hear or feel. I could not tell you this any more than I could tell an extra-terrestrial being what they definitely will encounter during their trip to planet earth, or tell a person what they definitely will encounter when they travel to an extraterrestrial planet. But being a deep-sea explorer of the internal universe myself, I can tell you what I *do* know about internal worlds. I can tell you the *trends* that

I see. I can tell you some of the things that I encounter within all people and this will help you to know a bit more about what to expect.

Journeying

When a person ingests a shamanic medicine, they often have their first experience of the separation between their consciousness (what some people call a soul) and their physical body. For example, when a person takes the shamanic medicine Ayahuasca, on a physical level, their body may be lying on a mat under a blanket all night and they may occasionally roll over and prop themselves up to vomit. But this is not what is happening with their consciousness. Their consciousness is on a journey. Their consciousness may be encountering giant snakes. It may be zooming out to see the truth about the origin of our universe and their place within it. They may be visiting the places that souls cross over through death. They may be reviewing their life, meeting extraterrestrials and the list goes on and on. But each experience is like a journey with a beginning and an end that has deep meaning to the journeyer. One of the most jarring things about shamanic journeys is coming back to the body and realizing that even though thousands of years worth of time could have passed during the journey, only a nighttime has passed for the body. Sometimes, you can't even relate to the life you were living yesterday anymore because of the perspective you now hold as a result of going into that journey.

The thing that advanced shamans know is that it does not take a shamanic medicine or a near death experience to separate one's consciousness from one's body. In fact, we can do it at will. Some of us who are more spiritually than physically inclined, do it unconsciously and unintentionally. In fact, the advanced shamans get to the point where they can project their own consciousness, having taken no medicine, into someone else's journey so as to guide them through their multidimensional experience. When you are daydreaming and you suddenly snap back to your body and where you are, your consciousness in fact detached from your physical body in the now. It was engaging instead with thought forms in the mental field (which is not physical and in fact is external to the brain).

The Connection Process is a form of journeying. Your body will be sitting still in one position, facing another person. To anyone watching from the physical dimension, it will look like you are simply meditating together with your eyes open. However, your consciousness is going to intentionally project itself into their inner universe and/or vice versa. The better you get at journeying, the more vivid and multisensory the experience will get. You will not be having the experience of meditating. You will be having the experience of taking a journey through the other person's internal world.

Imagination and Intuition

When we are young, we do not have the same attachment to "reality" that we do as adults. This is why we are so good at games of pretend when we are younger. Do you remember if you imagined you were a horse when you were young, you could feel your fur, you could feel yourself running at 30 miles an hour. Your parents were stable assistants. It was so real that you did not call it pretend. As you got older, the adults in your reality started to expect you to stop 'being a kid'. They expected you to buy into their idea of what is real and not real. They expected you to get your head out of the clouds and start excelling and buying into the physical world. They did this to try to help you succeed at life in the way that they saw success. But this is when you started losing your imagination and as a result losing your intuition.

Intuition is defined as *immediate insight or understanding without conscious reasoning.* When we, as people begin the process of learning to listen to and heed our own intuition, we often hit several roadblocks along the way. We often receive negative messages from our parents, teachers, or peers at which point we begin to doubt our own intuition. Our intuition gets obscured by the fears and beliefs that we have erected in front of it. When we lose trust in our intuitive knowledge, we begin to close down that channel of information by ignoring it. The good news is, though we may shut out the messages we receive from the higher self, the higher self continues to give them so it is impossible to completely lose the ability to be intuitive.

To be intuitive is to be fully perceptive, even beyond the physical dimension. To truly listen for intuition means to listen with all of your senses. Intuitive messages come in many ways and they come differently to different people. You may hear them or see them. You may just "know" them. You may get a physical sensation such as a chill or a hot flash or feel them emotionally. As you practice listening and honoring your intuition, you will get better at recognizing the ways by which you receive intuitive information, no matter what form it may appear in.

Your intuition is a sense that goes beyond the physical dimension. For example, if an intuition is about the future, the future has not happened yet. So your physical eyes and ears, which are here and now, cannot verify the validity of that intuition. This is a problem if you believe what is physical is all that is real. It means anything but what is physical will be discounted, ignored and disbelieved in. This means, you will not be able to receive any information intuitively. But think about this, if something that is beyond the physical dimension (which a person's internal universe is) comes to you, it is not going to appear to you physically. This is why there is such an intense link between imagination and intuition. If intuitive information, something beyond the body, comes to you in the form of seeing it, you will not see it with your physical eyes, you will see it in your mind's eye. It will feel to you like what your parents called 'imagination'. And you have already been trained that whatever is imagined is not 'real'. But it is. It is very much real beyond the physical dimension and something that is focused on that is outside this dimension can easily become real. Flight was imagination before it was imagined so much that flight became possible through the invention of the airplane in our physical reality. For this reason, in order to re-open to our intuition, we must tear down the obsession we have with our limited understanding about what is 'real'. For this reason, we have to welcome back our imagination. Much of what will happen during The Connection Process for beginners, will feel like something you are 'imagining' and in your mind imagining means something you are making up, instead of something that you are perceiving.

As you journey into someone, you will be seeing their internal world through your mind's eye, just like a visualization experience that exists separate from you and inside someone else that you are now perceiving. You will be feeling the way their internal world feels emotionally. These experiences may translate through to your physical body and you may start experiencing chills, hot flashes or even intense somatic hallucinations. Knowing about their internal world will often intuitively drop into you like insight out of nowhere. The inspiration to add something to their internal world or say something to someone or something inside their internal world may arise. The thing to understand is that in the beginning, The Connection Process is first and foremost an intuitive journey. As you practice journeying, the experience becomes much more than an intuitive exercise. It becomes an out of body experience where your consciousness actually leaves your body and you travel through the other person's internal universe with every bit as much 'realness' as you would feel if I actually put your body into a submarine and lowered you into the depths of the deep sea.

The Inner Universe

The inner universe is composed of two types of structures, walls and landscapes. A wall is a structure that is usually designed to protect the landscapes within a person. A landscape is the substance of what makes up a person. Together, the walls and landscapes will feel like *layers*. These layers are in fact the layers of the human ego. They are the layers of this person's identity. Identity is the condition of being oneself. One … separate self. Another word for this is ego. You cannot have a sense of self without also simultaneously having a sense of other. Identity served universal expansion because Source (otherwise known as united consciousness) could not become conscious of itself from a platform of non-identity. There was no contrast inherent in that. Oneness cannot comprehend oneness except from a vantage point of separation. Just like a fish cannot conceive of water until it has experienced air. And so, identity was conceived. A more practical way of explaining this as it relates to you is that the separate self, or the ego, is the necessary condition for you to experience oneness or enlightenment.

Whenever we associate something with our self, we identify with it. It becomes part of us. We make it the same as us. This is what attachment really is. It is identification. One could argue that identification is a good thing when we identify with things that cause us to feel good. But the thing is, the minute we identify with something that causes us to feel good, it contains within it the seeds of its own opposite. Worthiness carries the seeds of unworthiness; excitement carries the seeds of disappointment. Far more troubling however, is that we often identify with things that cause us to feel bad and as such, we must keep those things alive in order to keep our own sense of self alive. *The layers within a person represent identifications.* Things that they decided are associated with them and therefore make up who they are … both consciously and subconsciously.

For a great many generations, the ego has been looked at as the number one enemy of spiritual progression. But I am going to tell you that the ego is not your enemy. In fact, it is a necessary tool. Without the ego, we could not be aware at all. And the ego is juicy. I want you to imagine the most beautiful fantasy landscape that you can imagine. In this place, you can eat the flower petals and they taste like candy. In this place, you can ride unicorns and live in a hobbit house with a community of friends. In this place, you can fly. This is one example of a potential landscape within a person's inner universe. This therefore, is part of their ego in this life. Now imagine a nightmare landscape, a place where you are drowning in quicksand and once it swallows you up, you will never be able to get free. You will be trapped there, unable to breath and being crushed for all time and eternity. This is another example of a potential landscape within a person's inner universe. This therefore is also a part of their ego in this life. Now pretend these two parts are just two of potentially millions of landscapes within them. Everything you encounter in the internal universe of a person tells you something about them. The ineffable beauty of the layers of a person's ego and the horror of the layers of a person's ego and everything in between makes the human ego the most captivating universe a person could explore.

Chances are some of you are feeling excited to try this out as if a whole new world of possibility has been opened to you. Chances are that others of you are starting to feel nervous. Know that this feeling of nervousness is normal. The first deep-sea explorers also felt this way when they were about to venture into uncharted waters with no idea of what they might experience. We are all terrified of vulnerability and intimacy exposes our vulnerability more than anything else on this planet. I encourage you not to bulldoze that fear of vulnerability. I do not encourage you to allow that fear of vulnerability to prevent you from taking these inner journeys. Instead, I encourage the aspect of you that is curious and that wants to explore, to pick up, hold and take care of the needs of that aspect of you that is afraid. Move forward into this process with your fear, not in spite of it. With that in mind, I am going to explain walls and landscapes more in depth.

Walls

A wall is a structure within a person's internal universe that is usually erected by the ego to keep aspects of itself safe. So much of a person's internal world is created through associations, so it is only natural that growing up in a human world, an energetic wall within a human would serve the same purpose as a wall in today's world serves. For example, lets imagine that someone wants to protect their innocence, they may have a wall made of metal with a window that you can see through but that prevents you from actually entering into that innocence. As you journey through the layers of a person, before you get to the layer of their innocence, you may run into this wall.

The most important thing to know about walls is that they exist to keep the landscapes within a person separated and secure. If I asked you, how do you get through a wall, you might immediately answer, "you can explode it with TNT" or something to that effect. What if I told you that doing that would keep a person's internal universe closed to you forever? Imagine you had a castle and I came up to the castle wall and I threw TNT at the wall. Would I be considered an enemy or a friend? Obviously I'd be considered an enemy. **The name of the game with each and every single wall is to be smart and caring enough to figure out what the wall needs in order for it to feel safe enough to let you in.** To know this, you have to question every wall. Why is it here? What does it want? What is it trying to prevent? The answers to these questions will come intuitively as well. But many of these answers are revealed in the very makeup of the wall itself. You must become an ally to the wall itself or to the landscape that the wall is trying to protect in order to be let through the wall. And these walls are so incredibly intelligent you will never be able to hide your true motives or fears from them. For example, if you mentally project to the wall that you want to be unconditionally present with the aspect it is keeping safe, when all you really want is to hurry and be done with the exercise, it will be felt as a lie. So don't bother trying to convince them of something that is not true. That will only lead to them distrusting you completely and often getting re-traumatized.

This process is a connection process. Like any relationship, it is about *we* instead of about *I*. To be genuinely in connection with someone, aspects of your own ego must die or be dis-identified with in order to merge with someone's internal world. So, do not be surprised when you find that to get deeper into someone's internal world and through these walls, you will be asked to face and let go of your need to preserve your sense of 'self'.

These walls are energetic in nature. Some people have many more than others and not all walls are created equal in terms of their tenacity. They will often feel like a 'push away' or something preventing you from seeing and hearing and feeling more into the person. You will perceive them mentally in the form of images in the mind's eye. You will perceive them emotionally. You will perceive them as sensations in the body or even simply know all about the wall without any of the other feelings or visual images. You could run into any kind of wall possible in existence but I am going to describe some common walls that you may run into within people.

Barrier Wall

This is the most obvious and straightforward kind of wall. It is designed to keep you out by simply being strong. The best example of this is a brick or stone or metal wall. These walls tend to be dense and hefty. They feel like a real barricade. Almost all people have a primary wall that is external to them. This is the energetic wall that even average people are describing when they say in every day vernacular that someone 'has a wall'. This wall protects the entire internal universe. It keeps people at a distance and prevents them from beginning the journey into the inner universe. This wall has to know your intentions.

Can You Be Present With Me Wall

This wall occurs in people who have not been allowed to have healthy boundaries and whom were not honored by people around them as individuals. They are terrified of violation and also of abandonment. The people in their lives were never really *with* them and instead, had a clear agenda relative to them. So this wall is a kind of stalemate where what the wall needs is for you to convey the message that you do not have an agenda. You literally just want to be with them (in this case with the wall itself). It needs to know that you are not going to force your way in and you are also not going to withdraw and abandon it if it does not let you in. This wall will test the authenticity of your commitment to being with it like this, not going in and not withdrawing. This wall may present as an actual typical wall or simply as an energy. But you will intuitively sense that this is what this wall needs. If you run into this kind of a wall, the most important thing you could do for the person you are journeying into is to let go of the need to journey into them and instead, care about repairing their trauma by staying in connection with this wall for a potentially indefinite amount of time. The wall will come down the minute it senses this commitment. But if you sit with it so that it will come down instead of so that you can be with it, it will never come down. If you spend an entire sitting with only this wall, that is incredibly healing.

Constrictor Wall

These walls are often shaped like funnels or like walls that close in around you. They are designed to get you to withdraw out of the fear of being crushed or compacted or stuck or kept. For example, in a funnel wall it will feel like you are going though a wormhole. But it gets tighter and tighter. You'll start to feel claustrophobic. But one of the best reactions you can have is to decide to let yourself liquefy. Lose your bodily integrity willingly because of your commitment to the connection with the other person and you will slip right out the bottom, like water. You have to not fight against this wall. Give into it completely. Your prerogative is to find a way to speak to the needs of this wall in a way that cause it to expand or to surrender to it by letting go of your need to stay intact as yourself to get through it.

Pain Wall

This wall is designed to keep you out by discouraging you with physical pain. I have seen broken glass walls where when you go near them with your consciousness, you start to see images of your arms and legs getting cut to pieces. I've seen needle walls where when you get close, you start to feel like thousands of needles are being stuck into you like a pincushion. I've seen fire walls where when you get near, you feel intense heat and you start to see or feel yourself burn to a crisp. These walls are common in people who have been sexually or physically abused in some way and whom want people to know how it felt. See what your intuition tells you is right to do with this wall. Sometimes, you need to let it take the pain out on you willingly. Sometimes you can offer understanding for the fact that this is actually the kind of pain the person is in and when you really get it in an empathetic and compassionate way, it will stop and you will be let in through immediately to the landscape it is protecting.

Scare Wall

This wall is designed to scare you off. These tend to be very visual in nature. The ones that are not visual usually come through as a feeling, like the feeling that something is watching you. The visual scare walls usually come in the form of images that the person has encountered in their human life that scared them. They can even come in the form of things they know scare *you*; things like clown faces, horror images, facial distortions, an open mouth with jagged sharp teeth, certain animals, etc … To penetrate this wall, you have to master your own fear and convince the wall that the fear you feel is not a comment on or reflection of something that is wrong with *it* specifically. You have to take care of your own fear, while not letting it cause you to withdraw. Like with most walls, you have to be willing to let go of the urge to self preserve in order to be in connection this deeply with someone.

Mirror Wall

Mirror walls are walls that reflect you. They are good at making you lose the difference between yourself and the other person. Often these mirrors are every direction you look. You don't know which way to go forward. One of the best ways to get through this wall is to dissolve yourself into all of them. Another strategy is to talk to the reflection in the mirror. You may in fact encounter the aspects of you that are causing this person to keep you out of their inner world to begin with. Whatever you do, do not break these mirrors.

Gauntlet Wall

The gauntlet wall is one of my favorite walls because it is so fun. Unlike the other walls, the aim of the game with these walls is to outsmart them and beat the game. It is as if this wall says, "fine, I will let you in … if you pass the test". I've seen gauntlet walls that are set up like giant chess games you have to win or puzzles you have to complete. But the most common gauntlet walls are like the prowess tests you would see in many 1990's films; for example, a row of swinging axes that you have to get through without being chopped to bits or elements like you would see from the game shows "Wipe Out" or "American Ninja Warrior".

Repulsion Wall

These walls are made to repel you through your own negative judgment of the wall. They are made to horrify or disgust you to the degree that you pull back. One of the most common examples of this wall is a 'corpse wall'. I see the corpse wall commonly in women who are pretty and whom are only valued for their looks. When you approach this wall, you will see the person's face distort into what looks like a mummy or dead, decaying flesh. It is as if this wall says "would you really want to be with me if I looked like this instead?" To get through this wall, you have to let yourself merge and blend into the decaying flesh as if you are lying on top of and sinking into a dead body. I have seen these repulsion walls take the form of anything that humans consider to be gross. I have seen vomit walls, poop walls, walls made of worms or other insects, walls that are simply a scent but so powerful that it paralyzes you, spit walls etc. This is the manifestation of the things that this person has judged as detestable in the world.

Repelling Wall

As the name suggests, this wall repels you. It is designed to really push you away. One example of this wall is an invisible force field wall. If you get close to it, you get thrown backwards. I have seen electric repelling walls. I've seen walls made of hands that collectively throw you backwards as well. It is pushing you away for a reason. You have to figure out why and what to change so that it has no desire or need to repel you in order to journey further.

Pinhole Wall

This wall, like a keyhole that you have no key to, makes you feel like you know there is a landscape on the other side, but the opening is so tiny you could never get through it. The key to this wall is to figure out what will enable it to want to expand.

Kill Wall

A kill wall is a wall that requires that you leave your identity behind completely in order to get inside. You have to be willing to die to connect with the person to get through this wall. It is the Romeo and Juliet approach to connection. These walls are present in people who have been incredibly badly hurt in life and could not express any rage, revenge or hatred in response to that hurt. These people secretly trust no one. They are so convinced that people pose a threat to them that they can only feel safer with them gone. This wall may initially present like a gauntlet wall or a pain wall but you will have the feeling that it predatorily wants to kill you. The response to have to this wall is to willingly let it kill you. Surrender to it completely.

Disintegrator Wall

The disintegrator wall, like a kill wall, also requires that you let go of your own identity and reality in order to progress deeper into connection. This wall often exists within people who are deeply lonely because the people in their life (often parents) were self absorbed and saw the children as a figment of their world instead of as separate people to be cherished as individuals. To get through this wall, you will have to accept seeing or feeling yourself disintegrate and let go of your current reality. It is not as violent and does not feel full of rage. Instead, this wall feels like it is sucking in, absorbing and disintegrating you, or wanting to take you somewhere. But you will fear what is to follow as you will feel you may lose yourself. The feeling of a disintegrator wall is a bit like the blue pill or the red pill moment in the movie 'The Matrix'. Sometimes these disintegrator walls actually do present with this kind of 'fork in the road' tests. These people were never seen and so they developed the idea that to be seen, someone would have to completely leave themselves and their reality behind willingly so as to not have any competing interests or competing reality.

You Don't See Me Wall

This wall is really tricky. If you run into this wall, you will suddenly become disinterested in continuing the process or distracted from the process. It is the wall designed to test whether someone really is able to commit and overcome their own resistance in order to focus enough to actually see the person. Often this wall will not present visually. It will present itself emotionally in both the journeyer and the person being journeyed into. Another thing that happens when people run into this wall is that they get tired. Essentially, the person is trying to protect themselves from letting people deeper by 'sifting out' the people who really do not have the commitment and desire necessary to connect and maintain that connection or commit. I have found this wall in every person who protects their own true self by acting in a way that keeps their vulnerability safe. For example, the class clown projects a certain personality to hide his social phobic side. Failing to respond to this wall by focusing and putting all your energy into really seeing and feeling what is inside the other person, re-traumatizes them and reinforces the beliefs they have about other people and connection.

Deflection wall

This wall is very common amongst people who have been injured by narcissistic people in the past or who have been made 'the problem' by people who were in fact causing the problem themselves. The whole purpose of this wall is to weed people out by saying "You need to face you before you face me". This wall will either present without an image, just as an emotion or it will present as something within them that calls up your own issues. For example, let's say you are terrified of snakes or of abandonment. When you are inside them, you will have the experience of being prevented from having the fortitude to continuing with the process by snakes or finding yourself in a position of abandonment. This will cause you to stop focusing on connecting with and really seeing, feeling and understanding the other person. Instead, it will cause you to disconnect and withdraw into focusing on yourself and your problems and your shortcomings. *Self-doubt is a very common experience that you will have if you run into this wall.* Self doubt about whether you are doing the process right, self doubt about whether you are good enough for them, self doubt about whether you can continue or not. What all this has in common is it refocuses you towards yourself. It is testing how self centered you really are. It proves you do not care enough about them to face yourself AND stay in connection with them. This wall is an awesome wall to run into for your own self-growth. It will show you your own greatest barrier to connection. Often times, people think they are dealing with a "you don't see me wall" when in fact they are dealing with this wall. One great trick I have found to make yourself an ally to this wall is to convey the message to the wall "'I see that this is my problem. But I care about connecting with you too much to disconnect and go focus on it. Can you show me how to solve it?"' Oftentimes, including them in helping you to heal your issue that stands in between you and connection, leads to a kind of shamanic journey inside them where they hold a key for you. By showing you this key, they in turn get the connection they have been wanting in someone who is brave enough to stay connected and face their own fears to do so.

Defender Wall

This wall is a wall that usually presents visually and emotionally. It shows up in the form of something or multiple things that are protecting the landscape beyond it. These are common in people who watched science fiction or fantasy films when they were young and longed to feel the safety of being defended. Some common defenders that I have seen are statues that shoot lasers out of their eyes or that come to life to crush you. I have seen ninja turtles, superman, batman and other superheroes. I have seen animals, like bears or horses or bats. I have also seen goblins, monsters and dragons. Any time you run into an element within a person that is directly protecting the person from you going deeper, like a bodyguard would, you have encountered a defender wall. The only way to get through this wall is to figure out how to make yourself a friend and ally to the thing or things defending the person.

One of the hardest things about The Connection Process and about connecting with someone in general is that it forces you to face your own fears. It forces you to grow as a person. We are not used to going into someone else or really letting them into us. **The thing you must know before going into a person is that when you withdraw and disconnect from**

someone when you run into a wall or anything else for that matter inside of a landscape, you re-traumatize them and it will cause them pain. Doing this reinforces all of the pain that caused the person to erect the wall in the first place. It reinforces the painful beliefs they have about other people and about connection. Think about someone journeying into you. Imagine they see something or feel something that makes them afraid or want to disconnect or to pull back from you. Think of the message that would send you about yourself. The name of the game when it comes to connecting with someone is that we need to provide them with a different experience than they have had relative to connection before. They need to feel someone loving them instead of rejecting them. They need to feel someone bravely going towards them and into them instead of succumbing to cowardice and deflecting that their cowardice is about something that is wrong about them. They need to feel someone who is absolutely committed to connecting with them, seeing them, feeling them and understanding them instead of having more important things to do or making them responsible for connecting.

Landscapes

Both walls and landscapes are part of the essence of a person's singular identity. The 'truth' of someone transcends both. I want you to imagine that every person begins as pure consciousness, which is pure potential. It is this pure consciousness that creates the layers of personality and it creates this personality in large part in response to what it encounters in the world. So imagine that each layer of a person's inner universe is like a painting or sculpture that is created by his or her own consciousness. Each one is an art piece that when put together, makes up the overall art piece that is a specific human being. Thinking of it this way will help you to comprehend the magnificence of each layer and the message it conveys about the person it belongs to.

If walls were the boxes containing and preserving mysteries, landscapes would be the mysteries within them. They are the juicy substance of a person's self. Landscapes are really the layers of a person's selfhood. I have decided to call them landscapes because if they present visually, they so often present as 'places' with elements and characters within them. For example, a cave is a place. Space is a place. The ocean is a place. A fantasyland is a place. Even a layer of sadness is still a place you can be stuck in. Being inside of something, like being mouse sized in the walls of a house, is still being in a place.

For the most part when you journey into a person, because they are a human being, they will identify with things that exist in their human life here on planet earth. This means for the vast majority of people, the layers you will encounter within them will be comprised of things that relate to life on planet earth. Even a fantasy landscape or an extraterrestrial landscape is usually a concept that relates to human creativity.

There is no way for me to tell you what landscapes you will find within a person and what you will find within those landscapes because the potential is absolutely limitless. Imagine that I were put to the task of describing every 'terrain' that is possible to see on just planet earth alone. Because you live on earth, you know that could include glacial valleys, high alpine mountains, meadows, jungle, beaches, sand dunes and the list goes on and on and terrain is just one type of place. These places can contain so many miles and so many elements that scientists can dedicate their whole life to studying just one area of them. So here is where your mind will be blown if you let it be … Each landscape can be as large and complex as our own universe. What if our own universe was just one landscape of many within God and what if we were just a character in it? Our own attachment to the 'rules of size' that apply to the physical dimension, disallows us from seeing the truth in the non-physical universe. This truth is that a person could be a trillion times smaller than the universe that he is a part of but he in and of himself could contain a universe or more. This is because size does not exist in actuality beyond the physical dimension.

A human being could never explore ALL of earth, even given several lifetimes. In the same way, it is impossible to fully explore ALL of another person. In relationships, we often fall into the illusion that we know someone and we get bored with them. This is in large part because we are in a surface relationship with them. We are in a relationship with an infinitesimal fraction of who they are. We cannot get bored with someone when we realize that given multiple lifetimes, we could never know them completely or explore them completely. Every day is nothing but an opportunity to know more of their inner universe and the same goes for yourself. For this reason, it would be wise to consider yourself a traveler. Only instead of being a world traveler, you are now a traveler of the internal worlds.

Some landscapes will not present visually as a place parse but more as layers of energy. You might see these layers as the actual image of a layer of energy that has color and texture and that feels a certain way emotionally. Still other layers do not present visually at all. They may come to you as the emotional feeling of overwhelming grief. You may be able to feel in your body in terms of sensations of how deep it goes, like the sensation of swimming over a lake that you know is very deep, even though you are not seeing anything in your mind's eye. When you have encountered these kinds of landscapes, it will feel like you are melting through a person's layers like a butter knife slowly melting through butter, as opposed to visually seeing yourself going through a tunnel to get into another landscape for example.

There is no telling how many layers are going to be within a person. I have met people with as little as three and people with over a hundred. I will say for the sake of your understanding that with physical humans, the average is 22. A single journey into someone may not take you through every one of these 22. If it does not, just know it is taking you to what needs to be seen, felt, heard and understood at this time. No journey will ever be the same. When you journey into someone more than once, you will most likely encounter some of the same elements and layers that you always do within them specifically, but the journey itself will be different every time. You will see different things, understand more about landscapes you've seen before, meet different characters, comprehend more about the person and see landscapes you may never have seen before. It's the same as it is when you go to a country you've been to before. Some things are the same every time you go back but the experience is always different and you'll see places within that country you've never seen before.

Often, if a landscape is not just a layer of a specific energy or specific emotion or specific substance (if it appears to be more of a 'place'), that landscape will most likely include other characters, people and things that belong to that landscape. For example, if someone has a fantasy landscape, that landscape may include fairies, unicorns, trolls, waterfalls, trees, and many, many places within that overall place.

Sometimes, landscapes will appear like scenes rather than places. For example, you may just see the image of a person getting killed or two people making love. You may see the scene of a terrifying face or a scene from a movie or a cat walking through a hallway or the image of a child crying on a swing set. These scenes are still landscapes. The scene or image is still a layer within the person. It still has something to tell you about the person.

I will give you a very small list of some of the landscapes I have seen within people so you can expand your mind to include more possibilities. I have seen fantasy scenes and worlds, science fiction scenes and worlds, places that exist on earth in real life like the coral reef, Mount Everest, the Sahara Desert, the jungle, New York City or a specific house. Rooms with no doors or windows, mirror rooms, cave systems, boats, trees, layers of pure emotional energy like sadness or depression or happiness or disappointment. Places of complete and totally darkness. Tiny places like inside the holes within baked French bread or inside snow globes or in fairy houses or inside geodes or inside flowers. Places inside other being's bodies, like inside someone or something's heart or mind or shell. Extraterrestrial landscapes and space landscapes. Abstract landscapes, where a landscape is merely representative of something and you know it because of intuitive knowing. For example, a layer of white light that you intuitively know represents someone's innocence. Scenes of the past or old stories like the Old West or the 1600s or Jesus's time or the 1920s or even before the earth was created. Cartoon scenes, comic book scenes, drawings or paintings. Landscapes with no emotional feeling or visual component, but that makes the hair stand up on your arm or make you feel very cold. Scenes from movies or books. Layers of nothing but elements like fire, water, soil or air. Scenes from people's memories, like their childhood. Landscapes that appear digital or electronic in nature. This list could go on forever.

When you are doing The Connection Process, it is important to remember that you are inside of another person's world. *This means, everything within a landscape is actually part of the person who that landscape belongs to. We are doing this process with the intention of connecting with and loving them. This means, if you encounter a monster or some other thing that you have a negative reaction to within a person, that is still part of them. So, imagine you find yourself in a landscape with a dangerous fire-breathing dragon. You may feel tempted to slay the dragon and save something from it. Don't, because the dragon is part of the person too. You would only be saving one part of the person, while condemning the other.* That does not heal the person, it only does further damage. It reinforces the damage that was already done when the person came into the world and learned that some aspects of him or her were acceptable and lovable and some were unacceptable and unlovable.

What Is Beyond the Walls
and Landscapes?

As you are journeying deeper and deeper into a person, you are getting closer and closer to their core self or their essence. In an earlier chapter, I explained that all things you see in this physical dimension are extensions of what we call Source or God. I explained that Source or God is a consciousness that is so all-inclusive that there is nothing in existence that is not part of it. I asked you to conceptualize of God or Source as static on a TV screen where the static is just potential energy. I said that you could call it potential energy because static is only the *potential* of an image. An image has not yet appeared and has not yet stood out against the backdrop of static. But once an image has begun to appear it is now differentiated from the rest of the static. You, the you that you call by your name, are like a part of the static that condenses into a singular shape and form that differentiates it from the rest of the static. So what happens when we try to find the core self or essence of the image on the TV screen? We arrive back at static.

Another analogy we could use is to think of Source or God as an octopus, where you are a leg of that octopus. If we traced backwards from the tentacle, we would arrive at the center of the octopus. When we dive deeper through the layers of the human identity, we get closer and closer to a person's essence, which is none other than the stream of consciousness that was projected forth from God or Source that *manifested as them* in this physical dimension. Beyond that, we arrive back at Source or God. It is as if we pierce through their individuality and anything that is temporary about them, back to the aspect of them creating it all. The aspect of them that is eternal and that lives in a state of oneness.

The vast majority of people who report back about having threaded their way through all the layers of identity and pierced through to the person's Source-Self, say it is very much like piercing through to deep space. But it is as if they can feel that the deep space itself is a being that is omnipotent and omniscient. They have the feeling of immediately being connected to the big picture of life itself and as if their singular life or even the singular life of the person they are journeying into is microscopic in the scope of the big picture. Everything is put into instant perspective. It is very much comparable to the experience people have on a shamanic medicine journeys when they are shown the truth of the universe, God and oneness. It is also comparable to the states you can reach during some forms of meditation. It is also comparable to what many people experience during near death experiences. It is comparable to these things because they all bring the consciousness of a person back to the same thing … Their Source.

It is at this point that you know that you have penetrated through the layers of someone. You have connected with each painting (layer) to the degree that the artist is revealed so to speak. It is the deepest form of intimacy and penetration. You have connected with them so deeply that you have taken your own stream of consciousness and threaded it completely through theirs back to the Source that gave rise to them and also to you. If you pay attention for it, you can actually feel that you have threaded through them. You will feel the vulnerability of their openness and willing receptivity to you. You will feel yourself penetrating them in a loving way. You will feel also that by doing so, it is impossible for you not to love them. As such, it is impossible not to have their best interests at heart. Because of this, mutual trust is achieved and you are in the deepest state of connection possible.

Unconditional Presence

All this being said, piercing through to someone's essence should not be the "goal" of journeying through someone. The reason for this is that people so desperately need unconditional presence. Unconditional presence is the experience of having someone being present with you, focused on you in deep connection no matter what and conditioned upon nothing. *Unconditional presence is true connection.* Having a goal in mind is totally the opposite of this. It is conditional presence. It is sending the message that I'm being present with you *so that* I can get to my goal that I want to get to.

So much of the emotional damage in our life is done because no one was unconditionally present with us. Those of us who have been on a spiritual path for a long time, often get on the spiritual path because we want to heal ourselves. If we are truly honest, the root of the real reason we want to heal ourselves is that we think if we do heal ourselves, people will want to be with us. We will get the connection we were so desperate for and that no one could give to us. But here is the catch, the minute you set the intention to heal, it means there is a thought behind it. That thought is: "I need to heal" something. This implies that you have to *change or fix* something about yourself, which means that you disapprove of something. The best way to damage yourself emotionally is to look at yourself through the lens of 'something needs to *change'*. You know how painful it is to have someone tell you that you are not OK the way you are and that you have to be different. This is what you really feel when you convey the message to yourself or to other people that you are not OK or that they are not OK and that you or them need to be different. If you approach yourself or someone else with an attitude of "I need to connect with you so that _____", you have just taken a serrated knife to a wound that is already there. So, what is the alternative? The alternative is to fall in love with journeying for the sake of the experience of journeying instead of the destination or an end goal.

Fall in love with connection for the sake of connecting with someone. Fall in love with seeing, feeling, hearing, experiencing and understanding someone for the sake of those things alone, not because doing that gets you somewhere or is a means to an end. Be with yourself and be with other people unconditionally. Nothing on earth feels better than connecting with someone who is so curious about you that they want to connect with you for the sake of the way it feels to do so. This is why falling in love with someone is the most unbeatable experience we can have on planet earth. Falling in love with someone, forces us to be unconditionally present with someone, and to want to be.

All of us know 'those travellers' who go to a foreign destination and load their schedule full of sites to see so they can check it off their list. When they see those sites, they are never really there. They never really immerse themselves in the experience of it. They watch at a distance so they can go home and say they did the trip. Using this analogy, if we are those places, most people in our lives are like this kind of traveler. They are never really there even when they are there. The Connection Process seeks to undo the trauma of that perpetual human condition and the incredible loneliness that it creates in one another.

As you engage in The Connection Process, let go of an end goal. Make the name of the game exploration and connection with their internal world. Make your intention be to see someone, feel them, be with them and understand them. Know that it does not matter how much of their internal world you see or do not see. What matters is your degree of unconditional presence to whatever you encounter in their internal world.

The Missing Mirror

When we are growing up, we learn what we are through the mirror of the world around us. We see our reflection externally in people's faces when they look at us, in the words they use about us and to us and in the actions we evoke in them. This is both positive and negative. If your mother looks at you lovingly and tells you that you are beautiful, you learn that you are beautiful. If you get angry and your father acknowledges your anger and helps you to regulate that emotion, you learn you can trust your own emotions and that they are valid and that you are bigger than your emotions. Conversely, if he shames you for them and says you should not feel that way, you learn that you cannot trust the way you feel, something is wrong with you because you are feeling something you should not be feeling and your emotions are bigger than you are. If you grow up in a society that does not accept you, you see yourself as a person who is bad and wrong. If your teacher writes an A+ on your math test, you learn that you are good at math. If your family does not interact with you even when you try to interact with them, you learn that you are invisible. Some parents see their children as extensions of themselves and they will not recognize any desire, trait, emotion or quality in their child that is not one that they themselves have. When this is the case, the child gives up on having an identity at all. They become what the people around them want and it goes on and on like this. We come to see ourselves and form our identity out of the reflection we get in the outside world.

As you can see, our knowing of ourselves is dependent on the world we grew up in. We remain unaware of any aspect of us that the external world does not reflect about us. It remains a part that is hidden in our internal world. In this day and age, most parents, caregivers and people in general do not understand the importance of mirroring. They do not understand how critical it is to mirror the formation of a person's self-concept and level of awareness. They either only mirror a small fraction of who a child is or they do not mirror at all and as a result, the world is suffering from a syndrome I call "The Missing Mirror". We do not have any clue who we really are, how we really feel, what we really think, what we really want and do not want, what we really like and do not like. Many of us are beautiful, but walk the earth thinking we are detestable. Because of the lack of mirroring we receive in childhood, our level of self-awareness is poor at best.

For this reason, as you are journeying through a person's internal walls and landscapes, one of the most healing things in the world is to reflect them. *To reflect, all you need to do is to allow yourself to hold a bodily posture that is congruent with whatever landscape you are experiencing and/or verbally narrate the experience you are having, what you are encountering and the intuitive information you are receiving as you journey through someone's walls and landscapes.* For example, if you are going through a cave system inside their internal landscape that felt lonely and cold, you could tell them this is what you are seeing. You could also let your body language slump to imply that you feel that loneliness and coldness or you could let your body reflect unconditional warmth and love for that coldness. This choice depends on which reflection you intuitively feel they need the most. **Keep in mind that any language or body language that implies a rejection of or aversion to any aspect of their internal world is a negative message that you are giving them about themselves. It is a negative reflection in the mirror**. Mirroring helps a person not only to be seen, felt, heard and understood, it also helps them to see, feel, hear and understand themselves. It is a way to bring the missing mirror back to life. It is a grand opportunity for self-awareness.

The Connection Process Steps

1. Decide together who is going first; who will be
    the receiver and who will be the journeyer. The
    receiver is going to be the one who opens up for the
    journeyer to spiritually enter them. The journeyer
    is going to spiritually venture into the receiver.

2. Choose a place with no distractions and sit down in
    front of one another cross-legged and across from
    each other. Take off all your jewelry; especially
    crystals, protective stones and leather. You want
    to be as open as possible with the other person,
    with no barriers between you. Feel free to decide
    whether to loosely connect your hands or arms with
    each other in a comfortable and relaxed way or to
    do this process without touching one another.

3. Close your eyes and begin to imagine or sense or
    feel yourself opening up to the other person. If you
    are a spiritually minded person, imagine each one
    of your chakras expanding to welcome them in.

Once you have held this state of openness as your intention for a while, imagine or sense or feel yourself breathing in the other person's energy through your mouth, but also through your body (if you are working with chakras, feel yourself breathing them in through each one of your chakras). Do this with the intention that you are drawing their energy deliberately into your core.

When you do this, begin to imagine, sense or feel your separate sense of self dissolving. In true connection, the ego (identity) ceases to exist. For some people, this and the steps to come will be a frightening experience. Because the ego often thinks that connection means that it will die. Know that it takes bravery. You can continue with your fear, not in spite of it.

4. Look at each other directly in the eyes, deep into the pupil of the eye. It is OK if you choose to focus on one specific eye or you can relax your gaze to look at both. The journeyer enters the receiver through the pupil of the eye as if sinking into a black hole. If you are the journeyer, imagine that you are taking yourself through their eye into their inner world. If this does not work well, alternatively, you can soften your gaze to their heart area and do the same thing. Remembering that the journey will begin to come to you in your mind's eye as impressions in

your mind and in your emotions empathically and in your body somatically.

5. The receiver focuses on inviting the journeyer in, breathing the journeyer in and imagining or sensing or feeling themselves opening up to take them in. The receiver simply focuses on allowing, surrender and on the feeling of the journeyer's presence entering them.

6. The journeyer focuses on using their consciousness to penetrate deeper and deeper into the person, like a being that is exploring a foreign planet. Curiosity and non-judgment are crucial. The journeyer may choose (depending on what they feel the receiver needs) to either let themselves match the frequency of whatever landscape they find themselves in or to project love and gratitude into whatever landscape they find themselves in. As they move deeper and deeper, they may stop to explore and interact with any of the walls or landscapes that they encounter.

To let yourself match the frequency of someone's landscapes is the highest form of compassion and understanding. For example, if you reach a landscape within a person of doom, let yourself fully feel that doom and become that doom so as to understand it completely as opposed to projecting love into that doom. This takes much more bravery and much more willingness to connect, but it can be incredibly healing. If you don't feel brave enough to do it, or if you feel the receiver needs love and positive focus more, simply project love and appreciation as you move deeper and deeper into connection and interact with this person's internal world.

If you (the journeyer) are struggling with your own fears, remind yourself that it is an option to let go of your own self interest for the time being and focus entirely on performing the journey in the interest of what the other person needs and meeting those needs. When this is the case, your ego sees you as the helper, which boosts your self-esteem and so the ego supports the mission instead of resists it.

7. The journeyer mirrors to the receiver what they are experiencing by narrating their experience and conveying any messages mentally, emotionally, energetically or verbally that they feel intuitively called to share at any point in the journey. This feedback will be inspired by the interactions and experiences they have in each landscape and with each wall. Remember, any messages that you feel intuitively called to give the receiver can be spoken in the mind or they can be spoken out loud. For example, if you run into a wall within a person that you feel is there because it does not want to let something in that it may lose, you can say out loud

to the receiver "I am never going to leave you". Simply know that one of the most healing things for a receiver is to be included in on what you, the journeyer are seeing and feeling and experiencing inside their internal world.

8. During this process, many of your walls or blockages (both the receiver's and the journeyers) will come up. These walls are belief patterns and emotional patterns that have resulted from life trauma experienced by the receiver and yourself. Most people fear one more than the other when it comes to being journeyed into vs. journeying into someone. These walls can be visual or mental or even just walls that you feel between you and the experience. You will both run into them. This is especially true because most people are multi layered, so as you enter into them you will experience layer after layer after layer. As you sink into deeper and deeper and deeper layers within them, some light, some dark, some positive feeling, some negative feeling, you will find that in front of some of these layers, are energetic and emotional walls.

When you encounter a wall within you or within the other person, your aim is to learn from it and to meet its needs so that it will willingly open for you. The thing that breaks down walls the very best is awareness. You need to know why the wall (which is a subconscious thing) is there. What is it trying to prevent? Why has it chosen this feeling or appearance? Let your intuition speak to you and hand you insights about each wall that you encounter. Subconscious walls cannot withstand consciousness. They usually begin the dissolve once we are conscious of them and their purpose.

You can then reassure the wall that it is OK to open or dissolve and express your intentions for journeying deeper. Then imagine, sense or feel it opening or dissolving in the way it needs to be opened or dissolved. It is a good idea if you are the journeyer to ask permission to go beyond the wall. Beware that some people will experience their walls being broken either by themselves or by the journeyer as a trauma, and so these walls should not be broken unless the wall directly asks for that. Instead, it should be *loved* into non-existence.

Some walls do not feel like walls at all, but more like anything that is preventing your progression deeper or forward into a person. If a wall absolutely does not want to come down, we need to honor that fact and allow it to be there instead of force our way in.

9. As you move through the landscapes within a person, the best way to go deeper and deeper is to melt

through them as the journeyer and for you to let the other melt through them if you're the receiver. You melt and allow melting by completely being willing to experience whatever sensations, feelings or sights you see.

For example, if you experience numbness, surrender to the experience of numbness and settle into the numbness without resisting it at all. If fear comes up, be present with the fear, like you are keeping it company and are open to feeling it completely, even letting it consume you. If you have an experience like encountering a monster, let yourself fully engage with the monster as opposed to running from it. Your question to yourself should be "How can I allow this experience I'm having or engage with it instead of merely observing it even more?" Keep breathing as you welcome the experience. If you feel resistance, you simply breathe while you remain completely unconditionally present with the feelings of resistance that you are feeling.

In the absence of resistance to the experience, which is staying with the experience no matter what for as long as it takes, it is as if your soul has nothing to come up against and so it melts through one layer to the next to the next to the next. A person who is afraid of feeling their own feelings will have a very hard time feeling other people's feelings.

Do not be alarmed if you experience severe visual distortions and feeling states during this exercise. It may at times feel like you are hallucinating. This is all normal so remember to allow it completely.

10. As the journeyer, you want to see and feel the receiver completely. You want to know them completely. As the receiver, you want to be seen, to be felt and understood completely. As fears come up, let them be there, let them occupy the space between you, as if you are both cradling each other's fears between you, taking care of the fragile trust between you.

11. Be present with the journey until you feel that you have both reached a spot where you intuitively feel a sense of completion for the particular session. There is no magic time line and there is no time limit when it comes to The Connection Process. Often, this happens when we have gone all the way through the person's layers back to their Source essence. Make sure that you do not stop or retreat until you have reached and explored the positive feeling layers that exist beneath the negative feeling layers. For example, say you are in a layer of anger or hatred, remain fully and completely with that layer within the person, stay with it as you sink down into the layer of innocence that is underneath it and spend time there, in that positive feeling layer

before you bring the journeying to a close. Many people carry barriers and beliefs that people cannot truly connect with them or will abandon them because of their darker layers, and so withdrawing from these layers will energetically re-traumatize the person.

Note: If you choose to, when you have completed your journey with someone, you may decide to switch roles and the journeyer becomes the receiver and the process is repeated. When you are done, you discuss what you each experienced. You begin to process what has occurred together. That being said, some journeys are far too intense for the journeyer or the receiver or both to immediately switch roles and do any more Connection Process. When this is the case, we have to let the experience sink in before trying to do another session.

Performing The Connection Process with Yourself

1. Choose a place with no distractions and sit down in front of a mirror. Sit close to it so that you can easily see the reflection in your own eyes but you are able to focus on your eyes and see your whole face. This is about the same distance as if you were sitting cross legged in front of someone. You can choose to do this process with clothes on or if you are really willing to be vulnerable, without clothes.

2. Close your eyes and begin to imagine or sense or feel that the image in the mirror on the opposite side of you is actually another you. Like a twin or a 3-D duplicate of yourself. Feel yourself opening up to this other person.

3. Look at the person in the mirror directly in the eyes. Focus deeply into the pupil of the eye. It is ok if you choose to focus on one specific eye or you

can relax your gaze to look at both. Begin to enter the person in the mirror through the pupil of their eyes as if sinking into a black hole. Begin to venture into their inner world. If this does not work well, alternatively, you can soften your gaze to their heart area and do the same thing. Remember that the journey will begin to come to you in your mind's eye as impressions in your mind and in your emotions empathically and in your body somatically.

Focus on using your consciousness to penetrate deeper and deeper into the person in the mirror, like a being that is exploring a foreign planet. Curiosity and non-judgment are crucial. You may choose (depending on what you feel that you need the most) to either let yourself match the frequency of whatever landscape you find yourself in or to project love and appreciation into whatever landscape you find yourself in. For example, if you reach a landscape of sadness within the person, let yourself fully feel that sadness and become that sadness so as to understand it completely as opposed to projecting love into that doom or conversely, you can simply project love into that sadness.

4. As you move deeper and deeper, you may choose to stop to explore and interact with any of the walls or landscapes that you encounter.

5. If you feel intuitively called to do so, you may convey any messages mentally, emotionally, energetically or verbally to the person in the mirror. These messages will be inspired by the interactions and experiences you have in each landscape and with each wall. Remember, any messages that you feel intuitively called to give to the person in the mirror can be spoken in the mind or they can be spoken out loud. For example, if you run into fear within the person in the mirror, you may be inspired to say out loud to them "I know you are scared because you feel unsafe".

6. When you encounter a wall within the person in the mirror, your aim is to learn from it and to meet its needs so that it will willingly open for you. The thing that breaks down walls the very best is awareness. You need to know why the wall is there. What is it trying to prevent? Why has it chosen this feeling or appearance? Let your intuition speak to you and hand you insights about each wall that you encounter. Subconscious walls cannot withstand consciousness. They usually begin the dissolve once you are conscious of them and their purpose.

   You can then reassure the wall that it is OK to let you in and express your intentions for journeying deeper. Then imagine, sense or feel it dissolving in the way it needs to be dissolved. Remember that you will experience the walls within the person in the mirror being broken by you, as self abuse and so these walls should not be broken unless the wall directly asks for that. Instead, it should be loved and its needs should be met. If a wall absolutely does not want to come down, we need to honor that fact and allow it to be there instead of force our way in.

7. As you move through the landscapes within the person in the mirror, the best way to get through them deeper and deeper is to melt through them. You will melt and allow melting by completely being willing to experience whatever sensations, feelings or sights you see.

    For example, if you experience anger, surrender to the experience of anger and settle into the anger without resisting it at all. If fear comes up, be present with the fear, like you are keeping it company and are open to feeling it completely, even letting it consume you. If you have an experience, like encountering a monster, let yourself fully engage with that monster as opposed to running from it. Your question to yourself should be "How can I allow this experience I am having or engage with it instead of merely observing it even more?" Keep breathing as you welcome the experience. If you feel resistance, you simply breathe while you remain completely unconditionally present with the feelings of resistance that you are feeling. Do not be alarmed if you experience severe visual distortions and feeling states during this exercise. It may at times feel like you are hallucinating. This is all normal so remember to allow it completely.

8. See and feel and hear the person in the mirror completely. You want to know them completely. As fears come up, let them be there, let them occupy the space between you and the mirror, as if you are both cradling that fear between you.

9. Be present with the journey until you feel that you have reached a spot where you intuitively feel a sense of completion for the particular session. There is no magic time line and there is no time limit when it comes to The Connection Process. Often, this happens when we have gone all the way through the person in the mirror's layers back to their Source essence. Make sure that you do not stop or retreat until you have reached and explored the positive feeling layers that exist beneath the negative feeling layers. For example, say you are in a layer of anger or hatred, remain fully and completely with that layer within the person and stay with it as you sink down into the layer of innocence that is underneath it and spend time there, in that positive feeling layer before you bring the journeying to a close. You may carry barriers and beliefs that people cannot truly

connect with you or will abandon you because of your darker layers, and so withdrawing from these layers will energetically re-traumatize you.

You may have noticed that I referred to the person in the mirror as "the person in the mirror" instead of yourself. I referred to your reflection as another person because we have so many judgments and projections and illusions about ourselves that if most of us approach this process as if the person in the mirror is ourselves, we will not see ourselves as clearly. We also tend to be much more critical, unloving, rejecting, self-abusive and in denial when we do not externalize the person in the mirror in this way. In turn externalizing the person in the mirror makes the process much easier. Simply know that anything you see within the inner world of the person in the mirror is actually inside you. Any messages you shared, is a message for yourself. You are actually exploring your own walls and landscapes. You are seeing the truth of yourself.

When people do The Connection Process on themselves in the mirror, they often feel much less lonely and much less anxious. The reason for this is that you are allowing your own presence to touch your internal world. We are doing this when our attention is focused inward as well, but we have a limited capacity for introspection and internally oriented presence. For this reason, giving our internal world presence in this externalized way is especially profound. Having this connection with our own internal world makes us much less afraid of going into other people's internal worlds as well as other people coming into our internal world.

Joining Someone Else's World

One of the challenges of writing about this process is that I could never describe this process in enough detail for you to fully understand it. It is something that must simply be experienced instead and then everything I have said will make sense. Know that each experience is unique because each person is unique.

The Connection Process is not something that should only be done just once. There may be people that we will journey into only once, but we could journey into someone and never see or feel all there is to see and feel inside them even if we were were given several lifetimes to do so.

Be prepared for your feelings and thoughts that reinforce your loneliness, isolation or loss to come up in the wake of this process. Connection flushes to the surface anything unlike itself so that it may be integrated into our conscious awareness. This is the path of healing, but the path of healing is not always a comfortable one. So it is important if you have shared this connection to really be there for each other in the wake of the experience.

Teal Swan

This is a sacred experience. It is to be treated with the utmost care. We are now trusted with the authentic truth of another human being. They have entered a vulnerable space so as to give themselves to us, both their power and their frailty. We must honor that trust or else we are not in a space of integrity.

Separation is the real hell on earth and the worst version of this hell is when we are physically surrounded by people, but we are emotionally or mentally isolated inside of ourselves. So many people on earth suffer in this way. The antidote to suffering is connection. It is the willingness to join people where they are, no matter whether they are in joy or in pain and be with them there unconditionally. To do this is to say, I do not care whether you are in rain or shine as long as I am with you. This is what we have always wanted. By doing The Connection Process, we are giving this gift to someone.

An In Depth Example of
The Connection Process
- The Cave Within

B ecause I could never explain even a fraction of the potential landscapes that you might find within a person, I have decided to simply offer an account of a connection process journey that I did with a man who attended my retreat center. This may give you a taste of what the experience can be like. Because I am able to astral project, this account will sound like I am literally there in these places within him. Keep in mind that at first, until you really train yourself to leave your identity and reality behind through dis-identification, it will be much more common that all of this journey will feel like it is taking place in your mind's eye and you will simply be focused on what is taking place in your mind's eye the whole time. Doing this will feel like becoming very involved in a movie on a screen instead of literally being transported into the movie itself, as is the case with astral projection or shamanic medicine journeys.

We sat down facing one another on the ground and I decided, due to his insecurity around intimacy, not to hold hands. We simply left our knees touching. I asked him to breathe for a few minutes and simply feel me being there with him and across from him. I asked him to focus on the feeling of our knees touching. When I could feel and see in his body language that he was softening into the feeling of me being there instead of resisting it, I started to push my energy towards him. The first thing I experienced was that it became hard to see him clearly. Almost like a mirage was in between us. I felt the same feeling in my stomach that I get when I see a no trespassing sign. I felt like I was up against a thick brick wall. This was a barrier wall and it was protecting him from anyone getting close enough to see his internal world. I had the desire to get through it but knew that this agenda of mine was not what he needed. At this point, I could see a brick wall in my mind's eye that was at least 40 feet high. I sat down beneath it and had the intuitive impulse to mentally project the message to him without actually speaking, 'You do not have to let me in. I want to see what is inside you, but you get to decide if that is what you want. I will not rush you. I am not going to go away if you never let me in and I am not going to violate you by finding a different way in. I can wait no matter how long it takes.' I spent two minutes like that. Being much more committed to him seeing my level of commitment to being with him than I was to needing to get inside him, suddenly, the wall vanished, I was in the tender space between that wall and his actual body. I could clearly see his face and his chest breathing and the pupils of his eyes.

In a slow and attuned way, watching for his reaction, I pushed the energy of my own mind and heart into the pupils of his eyes. The first thing I felt was a layer of fear. It did not look like anything. It felt about three feet deep if I had to put a number to it. It felt like static. Being inside this layer of fear I could feel that it was a particular type of fear. It is the fear when someone has managed to get into a place where you do not want them to be in, but you are also afraid of the consequences of doing anything about it. It was the kind of fear that makes you frozen, waiting for what the next move is going to be. Like you are on guard but with no exit plan. I felt the urge to speak and spoke out loud to him, 'I can see that you are frozen and not knowing what I am going to do with you. You do not have to trust me. I do not think it is fair after the life you have experienced to ask you to trust me. Let it be my responsibility to prove it to you.' I sent the energy of 'letting him off the hook of having to trust me'. Immediately, I encountered a pain wall.

This pain wall was made of fire. It was vicious and blue white. It was predatory and wanted to punish and take out its rage on me. I could feel the hint of pain behind this wall. I decided that I wanted to take care of that pain behind this wall so much that I stood where I was and opened my arms and gave myself to the fire. It went into my nostrils and mouth and seared my lungs. I could feel it trying to scorch me. I waited for it to completely burn me up, but my allowing of the fire made it diminish. It was almost wilting to a flicker and then to nothing but a tiny whisper of smoke.

I walked through it into a landscape of pain. It was bitter cold darkness. But that darkness had a frailty to it. I got the knowing through my mind that this aspect of him does not know why life and love has to be so hard. That was the pain behind the rage. His absolute powerless discouragement that no matter how hard he tries, his relationships continue to be filled with inevitable loss and conflict and because he cannot figure out what to do to remedy it or even why it is happening. He is helpless to have love, closeness, security and those warm things he wants so badly. When I received that knowing, I told him what I was seeing out loud (mirroring for him what was inside his internal world). Sitting there in front of me physically, he immediately started crying. I told him to let himself cry. I told him that no one should ever have to feel that way and that it is right to feel so confused and in despair when you do not know how to get what you want more than anything in the world. We sat unconditionally with this pain. I imagined myself growing large enough to cradle that cold darkness, his pain.

Slowly, the darkness dissolved into the most vivid, pearlescent white color. It felt like the birth of a star, but softer and gentler. Behind that pain, with no wall in between, was the aspect of him that came into this life with innocence and pure potential and nothing but enthusiasm for what wonders life held. It was a layer of his inner child. It did not feel fragile at first. It felt magnificent, like an all-consuming benevolence. I saw the image of a swing set. I saw the image of him as a little boy, asking his father to play with a Lego set and I saw his dad reject the offer because he was on the phone. His inner being was showing me what happened to that innocence within him. I understood. In response to that understanding, I felt myself falling down through the floor of this memory I was looking at within him.

Falling through the floor, I felt like I was in a passageway, but that passageway got smaller and smaller and smaller. It was a constrictor wall, another test for me. I could feel this wall not wanting to let me further for distrust of me, but wanting to hold me there forever, stuck, so I would never leave. I intuitively knew I should let the part of him (this wall) that wants to keep me stuck forever, keep me. I said out loud to him, 'You can keep me inside you if you want. I do not want to go anywhere.' The passageway held me there as if testing me in what I had said, then, instead of having to willingly turn myself into liquid or some other substance that could slide through, or even having to let go of my identity to get further, the passageway opened up and I fell out the other side violently.

This landscape was very, very cold. The floor was dirt, but it felt like cold clay underfoot. It was very much an earthly place. I imagined a torch in my hands and one appeared. With its light I could see that I was in a claustrophobic cave system. It felt really foreboding. I had no idea how to get out or where I was in the system. So I closed my eyes and felt for what direction I should go. I intuitively felt I should go right. I followed the torchlight, which only projected about three feet. I was basically following my own feet towards who knows what. My hands were starting to go numb. A few steps later, to my horror, I was stepping in a small river of blood on a cave floor. I could feel the horror in my body. I knew it was my reaction. That horror was not something I was perceiving inside him. This is a repelling judgment about him. I knew that horror was not a reaction that was good for him. It was the opposite of unconditional presence. Instead of trying to understand this element in his internal world, I was negatively appraising his internal world. I stopped for a moment and talked to myself while staying inside him in the scene. I mentally said to myself, 'The reaction you are having to this is totally natural given what you experienced in this life. Remember that this is symbolic of something about him that needs to be seen. You are not actually in a cave. You are inside a man's internal world trying to understand him completely.' That was enough to make me feel curious again and also courageous to move forward.

As I walked further, I started to have to step over severed body parts. Reminding myself that I had to understand why I was seeing this, I kept going over them and felt myself release resistance to the fact that the bottom of my jeans were getting soaked in blood. I gave up on keeping myself clean, which felt good. The smaller passageway of this cave opened up into a larger cavern. When I held the torch up high, I could see a tiny boy sitting in the corner of the cave. I intuitively knew this was another inner child self of the man. This child was crying and terrified and covering his eyes and ears by being tucked into a ball. I felt compassion and then horror again when I saw that on the opposite side of the cave, was a giant monster. It was the ice monster (Wampa) from the movie star wars. It was eating half of a woman's body and throwing away the limbs, like a person would throw aside a chicken bone. Knowing what I know about the inner worlds, I knew that this was not only symbolic of how an aspect of him felt towards life and symbolic of his fear, I also knew that the Wampa monster was in fact part of him as well. It is a part of him that he has denied. I knew I was watching two aspects of him that were at war juxtaposed to one another. This is quite common when you are dealing with a person who is self abusive (which this man was).

I paused to catch my breath and really try to intuit what the next move should be. What did this man need? I decided to create a separation like a force field in between the monster and the little boy. I thought of it and it appeared. Then I talked to the little boy. I was describing this entire scene that I saw out loud to the man as he sat in front of me, like a narrator. I held the boy and comforted him and validated his feelings of terror and apologized that he has been stuck in there unable to move for so long without anyone looking for him. When the boy felt a bit of relief, I placed him in the arms of an angel (who I called into the room). I then went over to the monster's side of the cave.

I was not afraid of the monster because I already understood it was actually just the split off aspect (fragment/inner Siamese twin) of the little boy in the cave. The monster did not speak. He did not come after me in any threatening way. Instead, the monster's answers came telepathically through my own mind. When I asked him what he was doing by eating all those people, to my surprise, he telepathically showed me that he was eating everyone in the little boy's life so that he would be safe. That is why he had not eaten the little boy. He was convinced that all the people in his life meant him harm and so he was going to deal with it by destroying them. This monster was this man's suppressed instinct to protect himself by destroying what poses a threat. This is a unanimous animalistic instinct. I knew that chances were that when he was little and in the act of first suppressing that aspect along with the aspect of him that was terrified, he had watched the movie Star Wars and the two parts of him had identified with both characters in the scene where the Wampa had imprisoned Luke Skywalker.

I thanked the monster for being so protective of the little boy. In response to that gratitude and to being recognized for what he was actually doing, his frenzy of eating bodies ceased. He sat still. I told him mentally that the little boy had no idea he was protecting him. I told him that the little boy had simply been watching body parts and blood fly everywhere and thought that he was next. The monster seemed very sad and desperate to make the miscommunication right. He felt guilty. I could feel his guilt in my body like a ton of bricks on my chest. I took the monster by the blood soaked paw and led him around the force field to where the boy was lying in the angel's arms. I explained with words to the little boy what the cave monster had actually been doing all along. The boy looked up from his hiding place. I could feel that the boy felt the shift in energy between them. I could feel the emotional distance between these two aspects get smaller and smaller. I acted as a translator for the boy to ask questions to the monster and for the monster to answer. Pretty soon, the warmth in the boy towards the monster was so great that the monster actually made him feel safe. He got up out of the angel's lap and walked over to hide in the fur underneath the monster's neck. I started crying (literally) and I let myself sit there and feel the harmony and resolve of the boy pulling at the monster's fur and rubbing his face against it as if this was his best friend. The protector he never had. I asked the boy if he wanted to stay there or what he wanted. The monster seemed to simply want to please the boy. Even though the monster's appearance remained the same, the monster had transformed energetically into a gentle giant of sorts. The boy said he wanted to leave the cave and leave all the people behind and go live in the forest with the monster. So as a party of four, we all walked back the way I had come and then further until we exited the cave.

When we exited the cave, the angel vanished. I watched the boy walk off with the monster, still holding on to his fur and feeling safe, like he had a best friend forever. When they disappeared into a thicket of trees, I looked around and realized I was in another landscape. This was probably still to this day one of the most beautiful landscapes I have ever seen. It was a fantasy landscape. The sky was brilliant purple. The mountains were made of deep, blue crystals that jutted into the sky like layered razor blades. In the sky, a tangerine colored aurora moved like vapor, as if surveying the land that belonged to it. The ground was entirely covered in foliage. When I reached down to touch it, the plants were as soft as rabbit fur. I could not believe it. I let myself run my hands across it for a long time. I intuitively knew that this place was huge. This landscape was as large as another world. I could feel the plentitude of alien and fantasy life forms there even though I could not see them. I thought to myself, if I go back into this man in the future, I want to come back here and explore. I could spend a lifetime here in this place. Here, the landscape itself was alive with the unique essence of this man. I got up and walked towards one of the mountains that was inviting me. Soon, it got hard to walk. I felt like I was being prevented from walking.

I looked down and my feet and lower legs had disappeared into the path. I was in sinking mud. But in this fantasy landscape, the mud did not need to be wet. It looked just like any other part of the trail, but I was being swallowed up by it. I felt the urge to get unstuck. But realized that my attempts to get unstuck would feel to the mud (also part of him) like I was pulling away. That is the opposite of connection. So I stopped. I felt into the mud to see if it had an emotion. It did. The emotion was the same as a kid wanting to keep a toy and not putting it down for fear of losing it. This was another layer (landscape) that I was entering into. The mud wanted to keep me. In the name of connection, I decided to let it. I decided to surrender and let it consume me completely. It took a long time. I reminded myself that in a fantasy landscape, I could breathe still when my head went under. I was stuck there. I could feel that the stuck feeling was actually a feeling that belonged to the both of us. It was not just my emotion; it was his emotion that he was showing me. Stuck in a layer of brown cement like mud with no escape. "I see that you're stuck … Let's be stuck together," I intuitively said out loud to the man. Again, he started crying. I stayed stuck and focused instead on how good it felt to be together, regardless of whether we were stuck or not, like it did not matter. It was as if I was feeling that for the both of us. An image appeared of me in this mud and the man in this mud. We were hugging one another with our whole bodies. We started sinking deeper because of the weight of the both of us together until we were no longer sinking through mud, we were sinking through water.

For what felt like ages, we sank together to the bottom of the ocean. At the bottom of this ocean, we could feel the weight of the water on top of us. It was not black, it was dusty blue. It was sadness. We were stuck in the sadness. At the bottom of the ocean, there was nowhere to go. It felt pointless to swim back to the surface. There was no way to break through the bottom of the ocean. I felt stuck again. I knew that this was how stuck he felt in his own sadness. The bottom of the ocean was another wall. It was a wall that de-manded patience. Again, I felt the need to respond to it in the same way that I had responded to the mud. By deciding not to care if we are stuck forever, because we are together. I said out loud again to the man, "I see that you are stuck in sadness, let's be stuck together. I would rather be stuck with you than free and alone." I felt myself holding him and then as if a trap door opened in the bottom of the ocean, I fell through the bottom of the ocean.

I felt dizzy. I felt so dizzy that I had to brace myself with my hands physically where I was sitting. I felt like I was spinning. Then I realized what was happening. I was tiny, fairy size and I was spiraling down the folds of a giant, velvety red rose. I let myself spiral. I let go as if I was on an amusement park ride. I felt sexually aroused because the feeling and fragrance of this place was romance. Eventually I landed in the center of the rose, like a room with a yellow cushion center. The pollen made me feel intoxicated by romantic love. The light barely snuck through the crimson petals. I thought to myself, 'This is what is inside this man, hidden beneath all the pain. Any woman would be lucky to belong to this place.'

I had been narrating everything I had been experiencing to the man who was now looking at me with extreme curiosity about what was inside him. He had touched on nearly every emotion possible so far. I was alone in this rose, immersed in the romance of this place, feeling him like an all-consuming presence when he entered the room. He was small, like me. He was wearing tall boots, and a perfectly tailored jacket as if he had walked out of the 1700s. The feeling that I got was that I had rescued him and now he was going to flip the tables on me. As he walked towards me in a straightforward manner, like a man in love, I marveled at how confident he seemed. I felt myself turn feminine and fragile in his presence. He was not diminished. He was triumphant. He scooped me up in his arms so he was carrying me. He walked towards the petal walls of the rose. When he hit me up against it, the petal gave way and we popped through into darkness.

This darkness was all knowing. This darkness was omniscient and omnipotent. This was his true essence. I knew I had pierced through to his Source stream. I spent a few minutes feeling this 'true self' behind it all, it seemed overjoyed to have me there. As if I was witnessing his greatest creation yet. I could feel myself going all the way through this man. I could feel the relief he had that someone … anyone … was now in and of him.

We stayed like that, holding the connectedness for at least ten minutes. Nothing else existed. Nothing else mattered. I told him verbally, "I am not going to leave you. So if or when you are ever ready, you can be the one to decide to pull back from me so I am looking at you instead of inside you." He hesitated a few minutes, feeling the pressure to release me. I felt this 'pressure' and told him he did not have to if he did not want to. That ensured him of our connection enough that he moved his head backwards and I let my consciousness slip out of him so again we were two people looking at one another, with our knees touching. He grabbed my hands. We sat there in connection but in our own respective bodies. I made sure to spend the rest of the day in close vicinity to him and available. Something in him had quieted. Something in him was satiated. I felt as if I had been gone on a journey for a hundred years. Despite the trouble of re adjusting to where we were for the rest of the day, I felt like I now had the memory of him, like a gift that cannot be erased or taken from me. We were connected. You cannot un-see someone. You cannot forget who they are once you really see them.

Reflection

About an hour after we finished The Connection Process, this man and I were sitting around the dinner table and he told the group what his impressions were of the experience. I will share only some of them here. He said that when he was young, he was the son of a violent army man who was not happy to be a father. He shared that he felt like his dad was on a mission to make him tough and resilient and the way he would do this is by repeatedly beating and shaming him. His mother would enable these episodes, often saying things like, "he is just stressed because of work." So she failed to protect him and in fact enabled the abuse to happen. Because he was an army kid, he was moving around all the time and could not keep any friends because of it. So, he retreated into fantasy. He read comics and fantasy books and watched movies so he could retreat into his own little world within the house and within the family. That was the best way he knew how to stay safe.

This man said that everything that happened during the process completely blew his mind. He could feel that I was inside him and he could feel the terror of knowing that. He said he felt totally naked and exposed but that another part of him felt like it was starving and finally got food for the first time. He was especially impacted by the scene in the cave with the Star Wars creature. He admitted that for a year, he coped with school by pretending that he was Luke Skywalker on a hostile planet to survive school and to survive the fact that his parents didn't really feel like his parents. He was terrified of the ice monster when he saw that movie and would have trouble switching the lights off in his room when he went to bed because of thoughts of that creature lurking in the darkness. What impacted him the most is that the intention of the cave monster was to keep him safe instead of to harm him. He could see that in relationships, he had turned into that monster that treated everyone like a threat to be eliminated. It was not until that day that he recognized that it was not an evil part of himself that was like his own father. It was simply the part of him that was trying to keep him safe in the only way it knew how.

This man also admitted that the feelings of wanting to be close to someone, especially romantically, is a part of him that he keeps hidden because he is so terrified of trusting people ever again after the pain he had experienced in so many relationships, starting with his parents.

The experience of The Connection Process is just as impactful for the person being journeyed into as it is for the person who is doing the journeying. It is a joint healing experience. Often when we journey into someone, we encounter experiences that offer a solution or a new perspective to the very thing that we, ourselves are struggling with. The same goes for someone traveling into us. By being seen, we have the opportunity to clearly see ourselves.

Connecting with Body, Emotion and Mind

You can think of a person as being a composite of three basic things: body, mind and emotion. Essence or what many people call spirit is beyond all of these levels because it in fact feeds into, creates and makes up the three levels of a person. We need connection at each of these levels. We need physical connection, mental connection, emotional connection and connection with our essence. When we feel lonely, often it is because we get no connection on one or more of these levels. For example, a person who is obese may feel they get no connection at a physical level. They may perceive that no one wants to connect with them physically, so there is a loneliness and a starvation at that level of being. A genius may feel like they get no connection at a mental level. The landscapes and walls that make up their mental level might be so beyond what is normal or even conceivable to most people that in order to 'attune' to it, people must confront their own fears and the limits of their own mind and a very few people are willing to do that. This creates a loneliness and a starvation for company at a mental level. A soldier may feel like they get no emotional connection. In their line of work, feelings and emotion might be seen as unacceptable and insignificant. People may pat each other on the back and even share ideas, but no one connects to them with the emotional level of their being. This creates a loneliness and a starvation at an emotional level.

One of the most powerful variations of The Connection Process that we can do with intention, is to do The Connection Process specifically on one of these three levels. To do this, we simply set the intention and attune to the specific aspect of the person that we want to journey into and allow the journey to follow that intention. For example, we may decide we want to connect to someone's body. We can decide to do this process on the whole of their physical body as an entity, or we could decide to do it on one specific part of them, like their heart or blood or skin or liver. We may feel at some point during the process that what they need is physical touch of some kind. We can ask them if they are open to receiving physical touch at this time in conjunction with taking our consciousness into their body. If they say yes, we can give them that touch that they are starving for. If they say no, we can simply progress with our consciousness alone, allowing our consciousness to be the thing that is touching their body.

Another example is that we can decide to connect with someone's essence. Experiencing someone's essence is a bit like experiencing a specific current within the ocean. On a felt based level, it will feel powerful and unique, however it is much closer to the frequency of Source itself and so it will feel omnipotent and eternal. A person's essence is the part of them that transcends who they are in this single life. It goes beyond their human identity in this life, beyond life and death. It contains multiple lifetimes and contains the big picture of their current life as well as why this singular life was chosen in the first place. This is what we are feeling when we say that we feel someone's soul.

Like anything, the more you practice this process, the easier it becomes. You will eventually get to the point where you do not need to sit down across from someone and extend a conscious effort in order to see their inner world unless you want to. Instead, their inner world will begin to come to you like an offering from the depths of their soul to yours. The minute you meet someone, you will see images and feel sensations and hear things that are part of their inner world. You will be able to journey into this world without them consciously knowing that you are even doing it. Do not worry however because it is not a violation. Those who do not wish to be discovered will make it known to you. It will be as easy to sense and see that lack of permission about them, as it is to see any other part of a person's personal truth. But people who do not wish to be discovered are the extreme rarity on this planet. Most people are desperate to be known and connected to, they just have no idea how to get other people to know them or to connect with them. But now … You do.

Connection as our Lifeblood

Connection is the number one human need. We need connection more than we need food and water. This is why when people lose someone they love, they often stop eating and drinking. But the way that our society has developed over thousands of years has made connection more and more difficult to establish and more and more difficult to maintain. As a result, it is rare that we get the connection that we need from people when we are young. We cannot find a way to directly get it so we find ourselves at a cross roads; either we disconnect from other people; or try to get connection in any round about way we can. If we choose the first option, we suffer the deprivation of that loveless condition and we perpetuate the suffering created by disconnection in the world. If we choose the second option, we live every minute of our lives trying to earn people's desire to connect with us. The list of strategies that we employ to get connection in a round about way is endless. We try to succeed and be the best so people will want to be connected to us. We put on a façade of only what we think other people want us to be so people will want to be connected to us. We manipulate people to have to stay connected with us, and the list goes on and on.

We cannot rest. We cannot be. Instead, the emptiness we feel, the emotional starvation, compels us to keep in motion. It compels us to constantly 'do' so as to make ourselves worthy of the connection that in fact should be ours whether we do anything or not. When none of our compulsive 'doing' works to get us the connection we need, we use doing as a means of escaping from that internal void that we feel. We use doing as a substitute for connection itself. But the reality is, no matter what we try to do to compensate for a lack of connection, it never works. The reality is, there never has been, isn't and never will be a substitute for connection.

Connection is not something that you can earn. Like the air that you breathe, it is a necessity of life itself. To earn connection means the person you earned that connection from was never there for connection to begin with. It means you were a means to an end for them. It means being connected with you got them something else that they wanted. It was never about you and it was not the value of the connection itself that they were getting from you.

Genuine connection is something that occurs for the sake of connection. It is something that happens for gift of the experience of closeness. It is for the gift of

the experience of seeing, hearing, feeling and understanding someone and being seen, being heard, being
felt and being understood in return.

Ultimately the number one desire, the desire that
hides beneath all other desires, is the desire for connection. Ultimately, what we all want is a world where we
are so interconnected that we can rest in the security
that we are all taking each other's best interests as part of
our own best interests. We want a world where we are
not alone. We want a world where we are seen, heard,
felt and understood deeply. To actualize this world that
we all want, we must take the initiative to become that
change we wish to see in the external world. We must
be willing to be brave enough to see, hear, feel and
understand ourselves. We must be willing to be brave
enough to see, hear, feel and understand each other.

Other Books By Teal Swan

Anatomy Of Loneliness

In The *Anatomy of Loneliness*, Teal identifies the three pillars or qualities of loneliness: Separation, Shame and Fear and goes on to share her revolutionary technique; The Connection Process, a form of intuitive journeying, usually involving two people a 'receiver' and a 'journeyer'. Through a series of exercises each person experiences 'walls' and 'blockages' as they move through the process both participants face their fears learning from these to reach a place of unconditional love and acceptance.

The Completion Process

The Completion Process takes readers along on her restorative journey of healing and liberation. For anyone who has been fractured by trauma—and according to Teal, in one way or another, we all have—here is a way to put ourselves back together again, no longer inhibited by the past or terrified of the future.

Drawing on her wide range of extrasensory abilities—including clairvoyance, clairsentience, and clairaudience—and incorporating key aspects of inner child and shadow work, Teal offers a revolutionary 20-step process for healing any past hurt or present problem.

Shadows Before Dawn

Teal documents how she dug herself out of self-hate into self-love, and details the remarkable trail for others to get to the same place. *Shadows Before Dawn* encompasses both Teal's compelling story, told with raw intensity, and her resolute, no-nonsense how-to guide to healing from even the deepest levels of suffering. Offering a comprehensive self-love tool kit, this book includes powerful exercises, insights, and perspective from a captivating new teacher in spirituality, and lets you pick and choose which techniques are right for you.

Teal's resonating words will sit with your soul long after you put this book down and will serve as guideposts on the way to complete self-love, no matter who you are or where you are in life

The Sculptor In The Sky

You can not have a life, you can not lose a life... You are life. It is you who hold the power to decide yourself back onto the path you intended... the path of welcoming and becoming your own bliss. *The Sculptor In The Sky*, the new book by spiritual catalyst, Teal Scott takes you on a journey of rediscovery of the universe of god and of yourself. This extraordinary book challenges us to reconnect with the eternal essence of our being and to expand our ideas about the reality we live in It is a must have for the curious, the wanting and the ready. A provocative guide to answering the questions that every person asks at some point in their life.

Teal Swan Frequency Paintings

These frequency images, created by Teal Swan, are paintings of the energetic, vibrational frequency (pre-manifestation) of the specific subject matter each one represents. By focusing on these images and having them in your living space, they will cause your energy to entrain with and resonate at the same frequency and amplitude of the vibration that they are created to convey. In turn, this aids you to amplify and manifest the presence of the subject matter in your life.

Teal Swan Frequency Tarot Deck

www.TealSwan.com/store

Teal Swan Frequency Clothing
Women - Men - Kids: T-Shirts - Dresses - Shoes - Leggings - Swimwear - Backpacks - Notebooks - And More!

www.FrequencyProduct.com